# Library

by Sheila Anderson

first step nonfiction

Lerner Publications Company · Minneapolis

There is a library in my community.

It has books.

It has movies.

It has computers.

It has reading spaces.

It has librarians.

Have you been to a library?